The Reggae Songbook

NOA

11-95

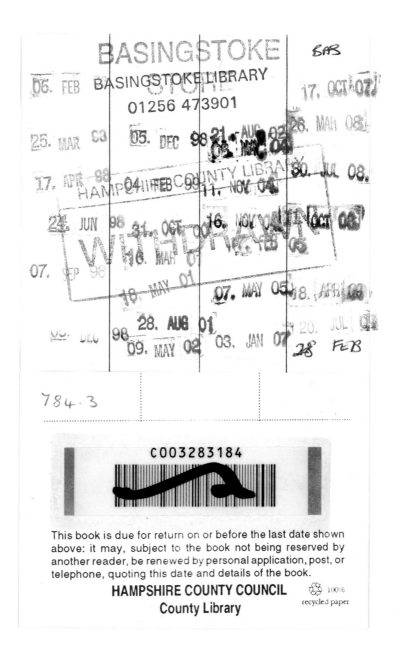

This book is due for return on or before the last date shown above: it may, subject to the book not being reserved by another reader, be renewed by personal application, post, or telephone, quoting this date and details of the book.

HAMPSHIRE COUNTY COUNCIL   100%
County Library   recycled paper

The Reggae Songbook

Sixteen of the best reggae songs ever!
Includes hits by UB40, Yellowman, Musical Youth, and many more!

AMSCO PUBLICATIONS

Cover design by Amy MacIntyre
Front cover photography by R. Deluze/Stills/Retna Ltd.

Back cover photography:
UB40 Pete Tangen/Retna Ltd.
10cc Vandervoohr/Retna Ltd.
Desmond Dekker King Collection/Retna Ltd.
Musical Youth Arain Boot/Retna Ltd.
The Wailers Steve Eichner/Retna Ltd.
Yellowman Lisa Haun/Retna Ltd.
Blondie Michael Putland/Retna Ltd.

Order No. AM 931392
US International Standard Book Number: 0.8256.1502.X
UK International Standard Book Number: 0.7119.5140.3

Exclusive Distributors:
Music Sales Corporation
257 Park Avenue South, New York, New York 10010 USA
Music Sales Limited
8/9 Frith Street, London W1V 5TZ England
Music Sales Pty. Limited
120 Rothschild Street, Rosebery, Sydney, NSW 2018, Australia

Printed in the United States of America by
Vicks Lithograph and Printing Corporation

BUFFALO SOLDIER

Words and Music by Bob Marley and Noel Williams

Moderate Shuffle

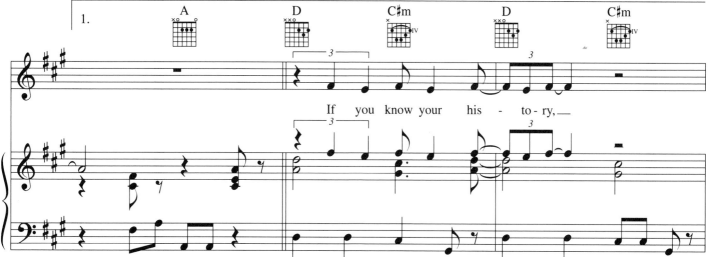

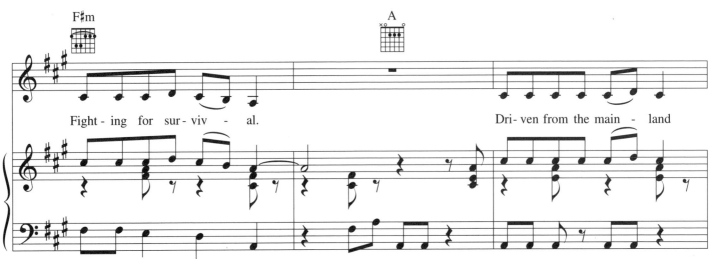

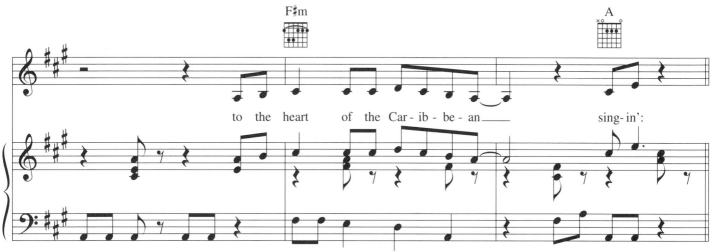

PASS THE DUTCHIE

Words and Music by Jackie Mittoo, Lloyd Ferguson, Fitzroy Simpson, Robbie Lynn,
Leroy Sibbles and Headley Bennett

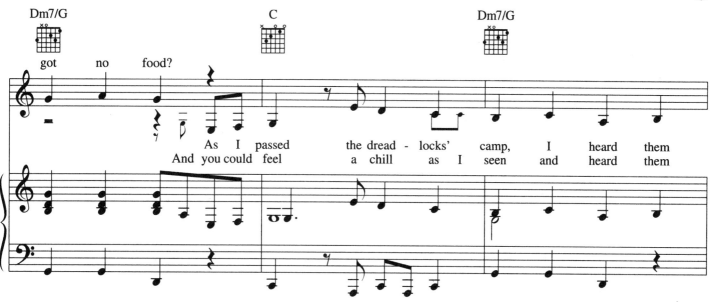

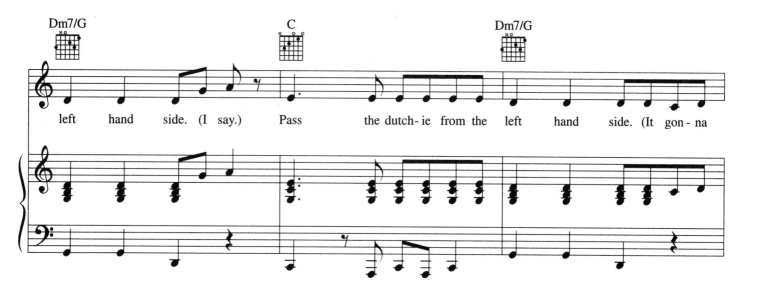

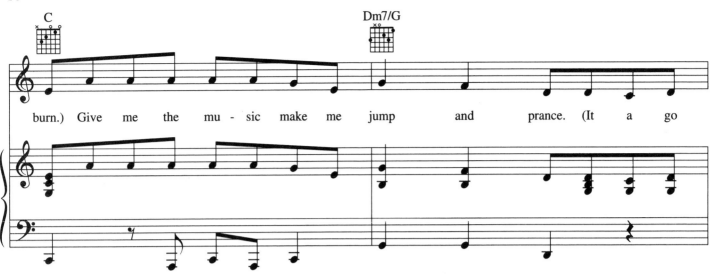

burn.) Give me the mu - sic make me jump and prance. (It a go

done.) Give me the mu - sic make me rock in at the dance. Bum

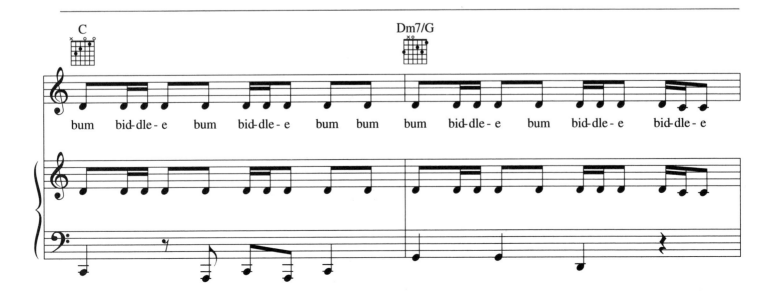

bum bid-dle - e bum bid-dle - e bum bum bum bid-dle - e bum bid-dle - e bid-dle - e

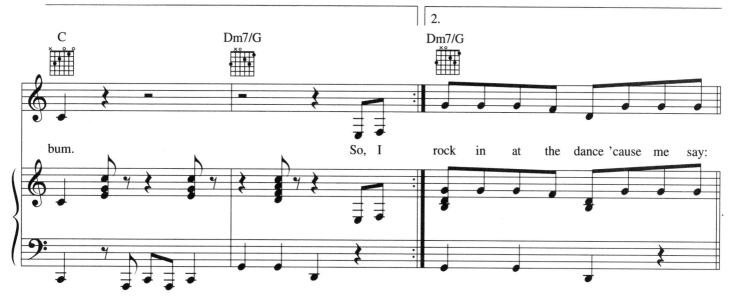

bum.   So, I rock in at the dance 'cause me say:

Lis - ten to the drum-mer. Me say: Lis-ten to the bass.   Give me lit - tle mu - sic make me

wind up   me waist.   Me say: wind up   me waist. I say:

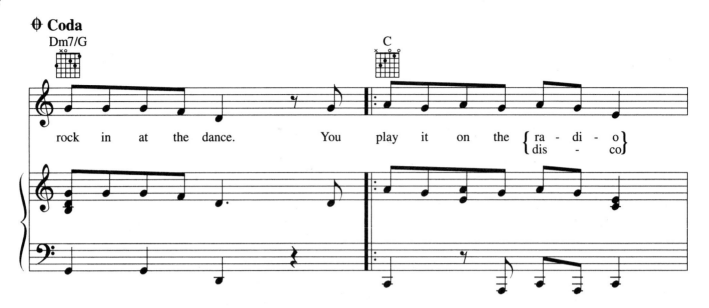

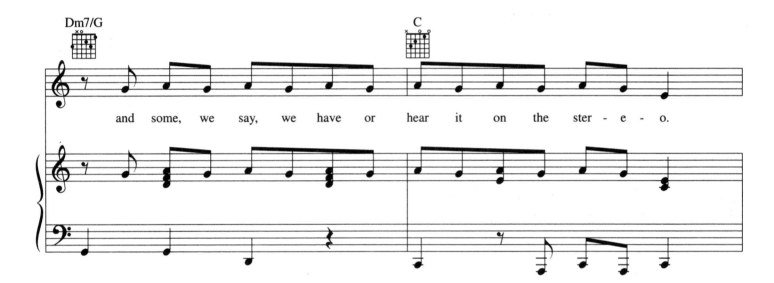

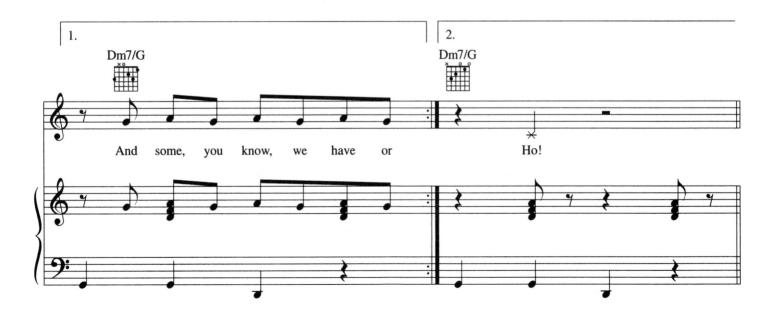

KINGSTON TOWN

Words and Music by Kenrick R. Patrick

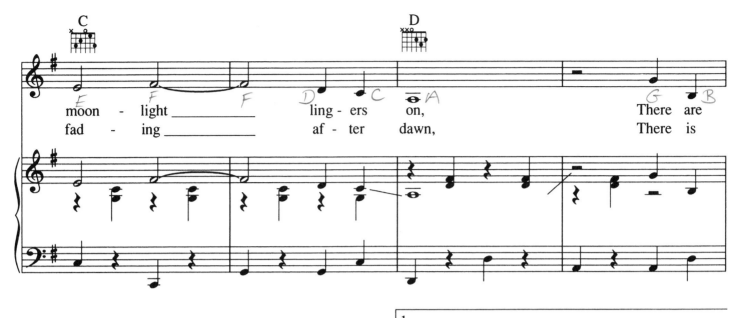

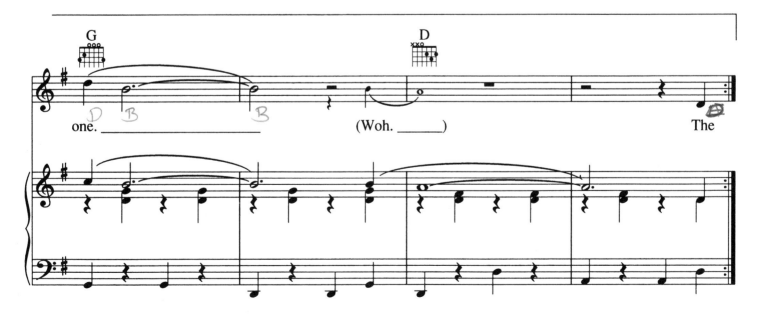

23

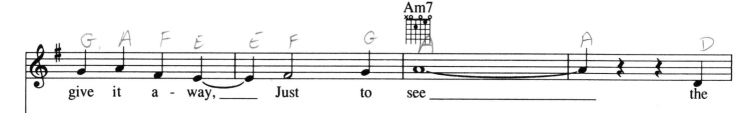

give it a-way,____ Just to see _____ the

girls _____ at play. _____

When _____ I am
now _____ I am

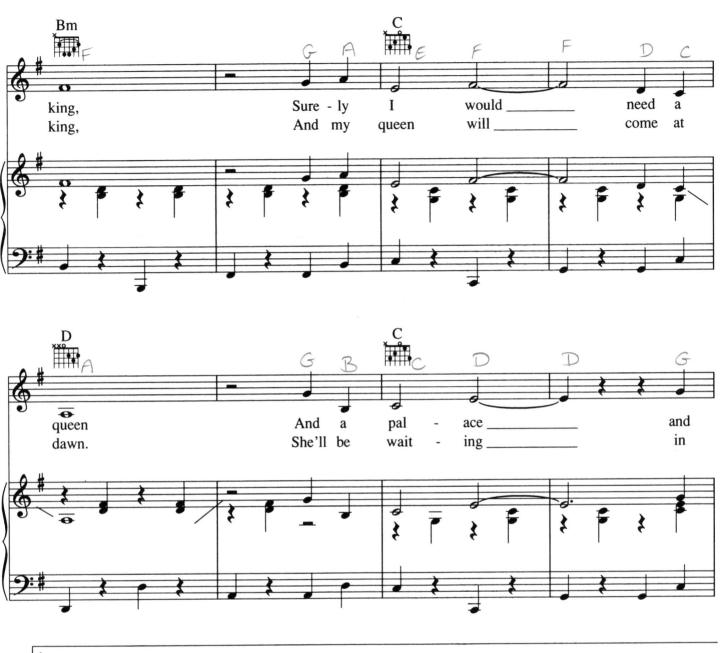

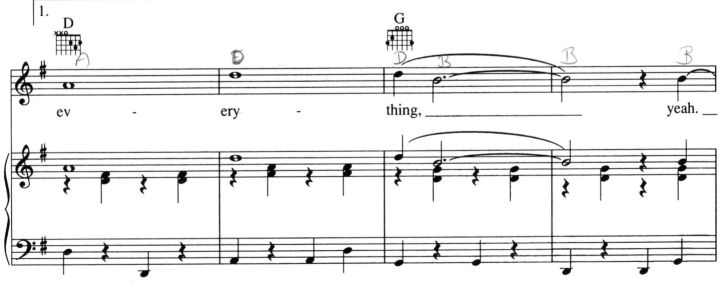

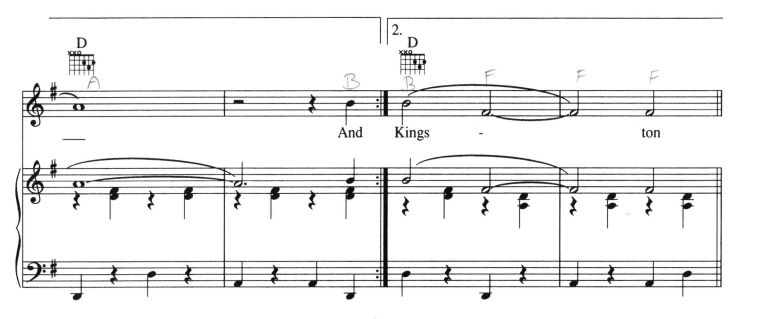

And Kings - ton

Town. _____ She'll be

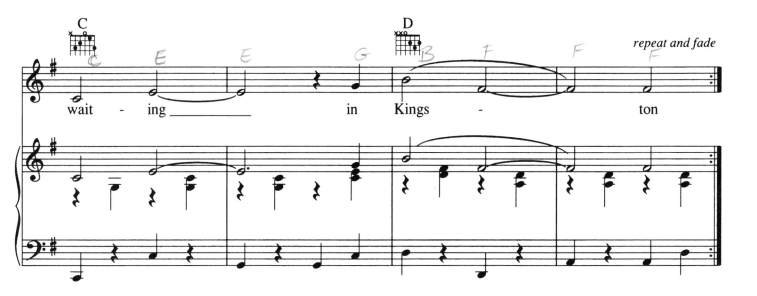

wait - ing _____ in Kings - ton

DREADLOCK HOLIDAY

Words and Music by Eric Stewart and Graham Gouldman

and I looked round in a state — of fright.
It was a pres - ent from me moth - er."
"Would you like some-thing hard - er?"

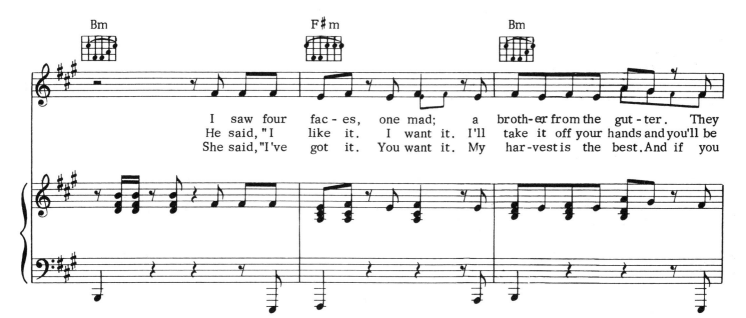

I saw four fac - es, one mad; a broth-er from the gut - ter. They
He said, "I like it. I want it. I'll take it off your hands and you'll be
She said, "I've got it. You want it. My har-vest is the best. And if you

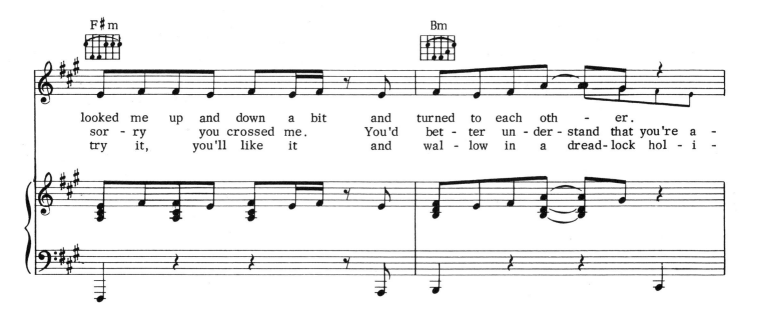

looked me up and down a bit and turned to each oth - er.
sor - ry you crossed me. You'd bet - ter un - der-stand that you're a -
try it, you'll like it and wal - low in a dread-lock hol - i -

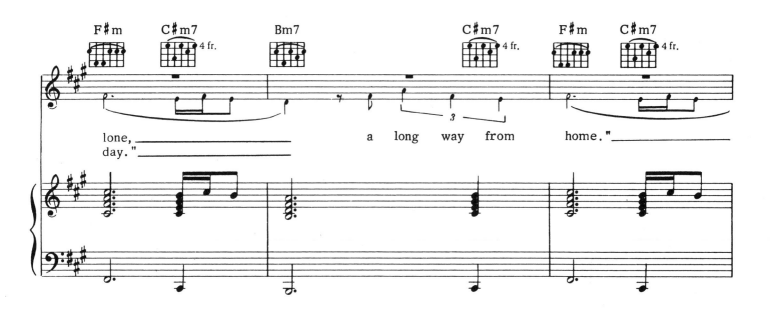

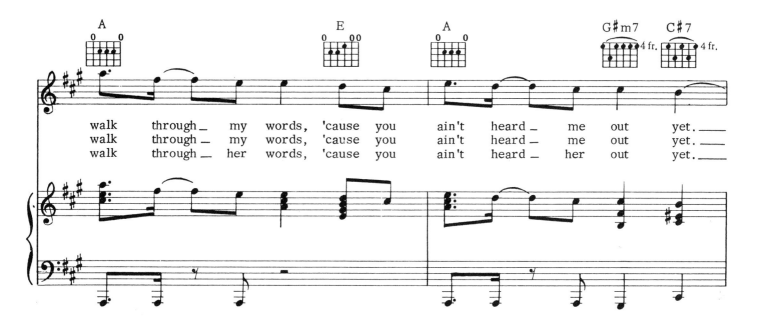

THE TIDE IS HIGH

Words and Music by John Holt

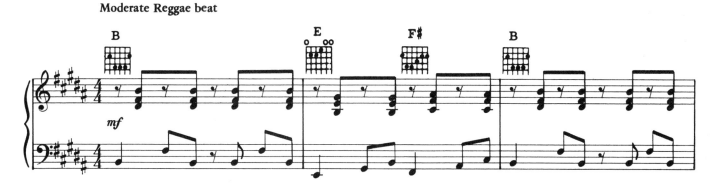

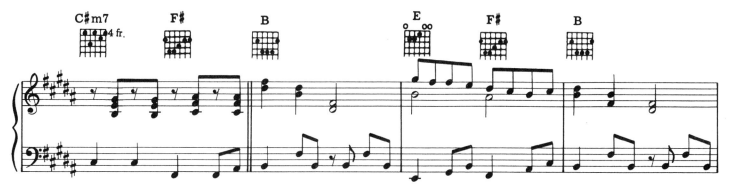

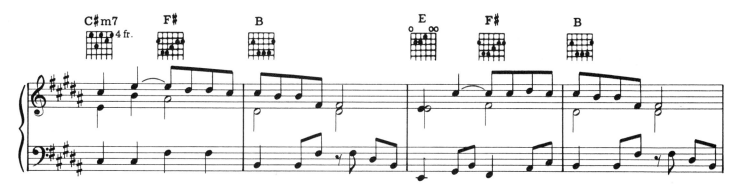

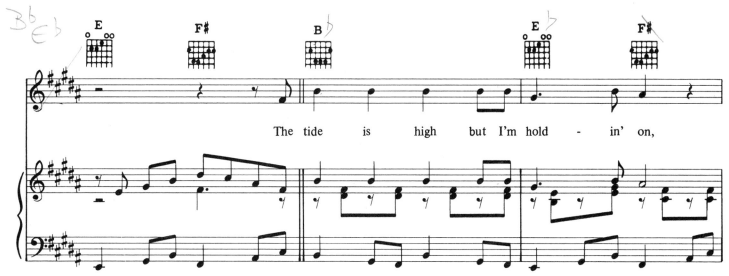

The tide is high but I'm hold - in' on,

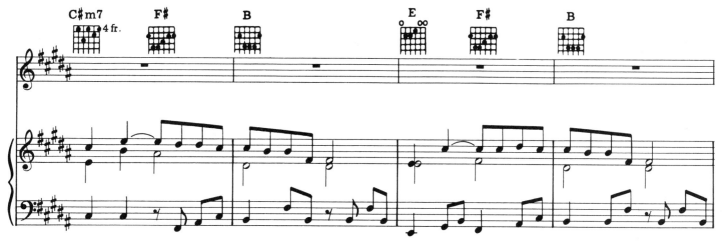

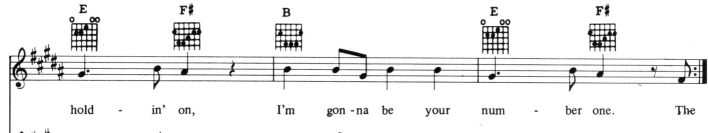

ANAREXOL

Words and Music by Ripton Hylton and Henry Lawes

42

BABY

Words and Music by L. Sibbles, B. Llewellyn and E. Morgan

Moderately bright

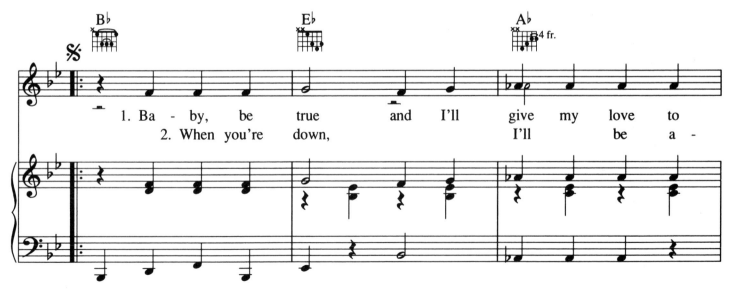

1. Ba - by, be true and I'll give my love to
2. When you're down, I'll be a -

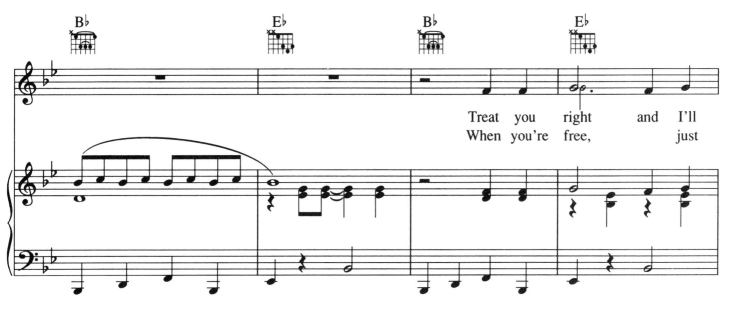

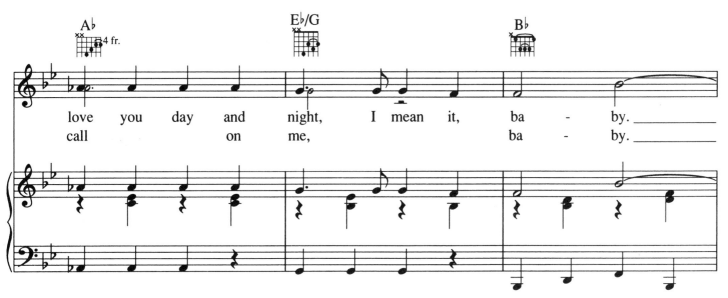

I'll give my world to
I'll give my heart to

you   now, babe.
you   now, babe.

I'll   do   what you ask ___ me

to   now,   babe.

I   mean   it,

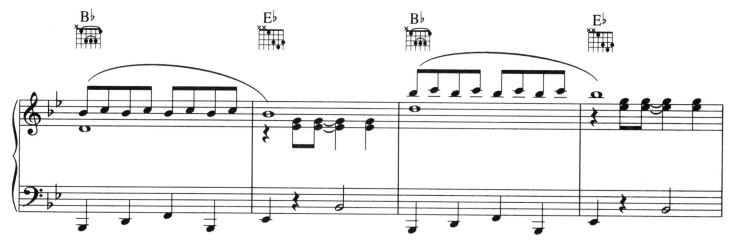

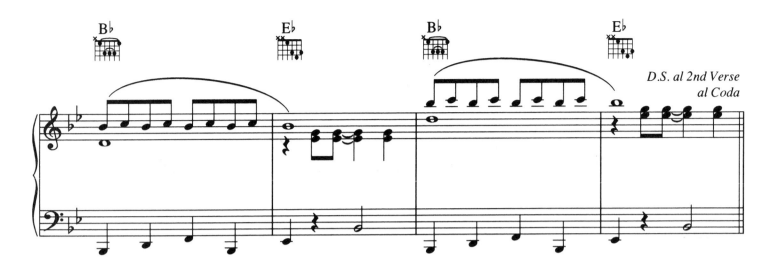

D.S. al 2nd Verse
al Coda

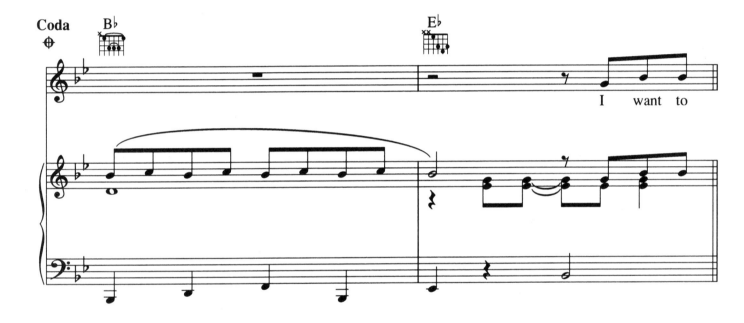

I want to

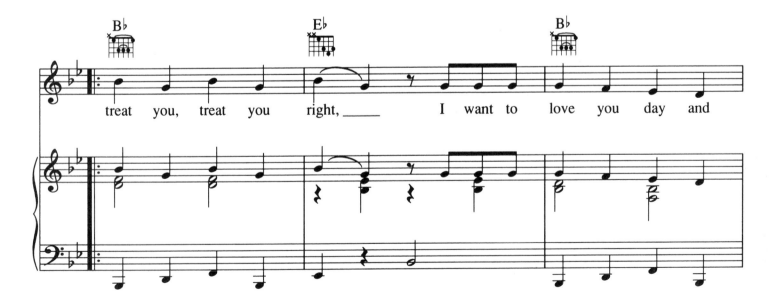

treat you, treat you right, _____ I want to love you day and

night. _____   I want to give my heart a - way,   I want to

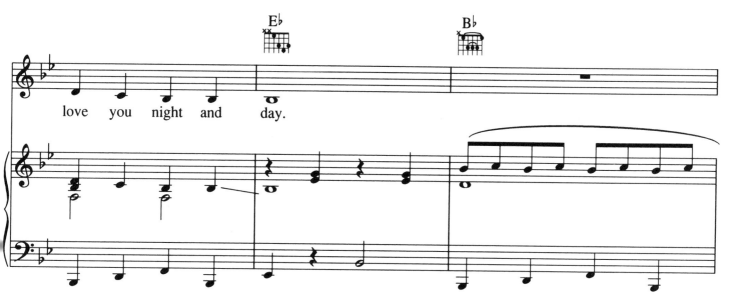

love you night and day.

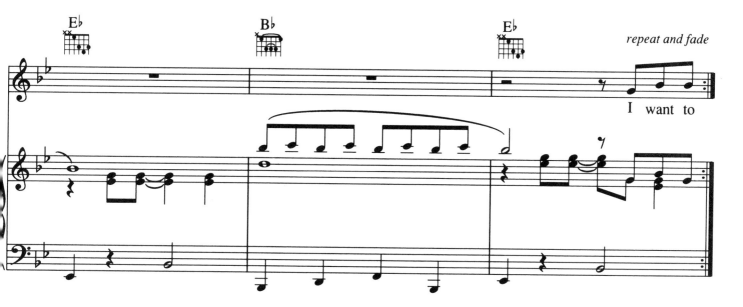

repeat and fade

I want to

HAPPY GO LUCKY GIRL

Words and Music by John Holt

Moderate reggae shuffle

how___ man - y pride you've broke. I - mag - ine

how___ man - y hearts___ you've stole._____

Ev-'ry-one in town

knows a-bout__ you,___ hap-py go luck - y girl.___

luck - y girl.

A - ha, a - ha, hap - py go

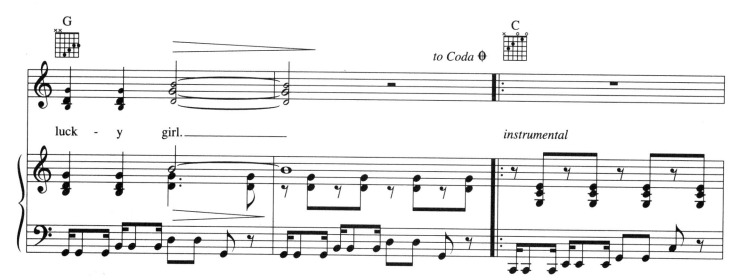

luck - y girl.

to Coda

instrumental

1.

54

THE ISRAELITES

Words and Music by Desmond Dacres and Leslie Kong

Moderate shuffle (♫ = ♩♪)

Get up in the morn- ing slav - ing for bread, sir, so that a ev- er- y mouth___

___ can be ___ fed. ___ Poor _____ me,

Is - rael- ite. ___ My wife and my kids, they packed

up and they leave me; "Dar- ling," she said, "I was yours___ to re - ceive."___

After a storm there must____ be a calm - ing. They catch me in the farm, you

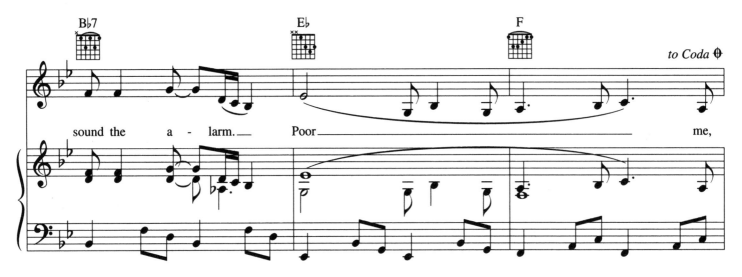

sound the a - larm.____ Poor_____ me,

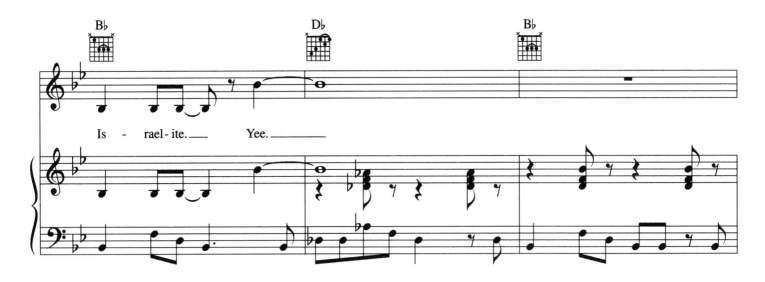

Is - rael - ite.____ Yee._____

MOUSE AND THE MAN

Words and Music by Ripton Hylton and Linval Thompson

MY PRECIOUS WORLD (THE MAN)

by Desmond Dacres and Leslie Kong

SHE CAUGHT THE TRAIN

Words and Music by Joe Monsano

Moderately, with a steady beat

An- oth- er night of lone- li - ness. My love is gone.

Doo doo doo doo. Doo doo doo

doo. Doo doo doo doo.

Doo doo doo doo.

repeat and fade

SIMMER DOWN

by Clem Dodd

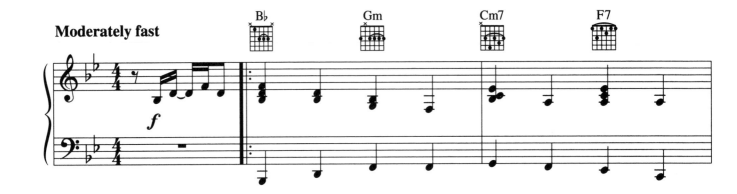

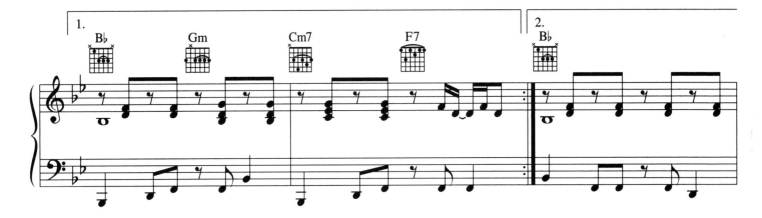

Sim - mer down. You're leav - ing in - to the high shore

RED, RED WINE

Words and Music by Neil Diamond

WEAR YOU TO THE BALL

Words and Music by John Holt

Moderately slow, with a steady beat

No chord

mf

C

Am

I'm gon - na wear you to the ball to - night.

G

C   **(Rap style)**

Put on your best dress to - night. Did you hear what the man said,

me soul broth-ers and give me soul sis - ters. Don't beg for no mer - cy.

Move it up, break it up. It's in the bot - tle, it's

good. She's got it. She's got it, she's got it, she's got it.

(Sung)

Though those _____ oth - er guys may put you down,

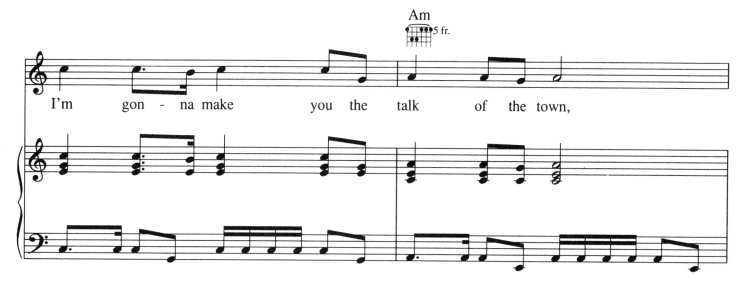

I'm gon - na make you the talk of the town,

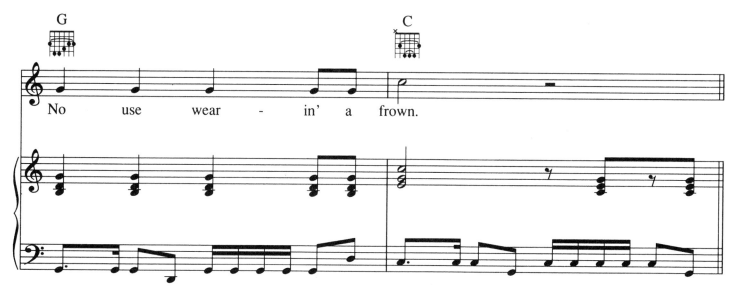

No use wear - in' a frown.

Instrumental solo

repeat and fade

ZUNGGUZUNGGUGUZUNGGUZENG

Words and Music by Winston Foster and Henry Lawes

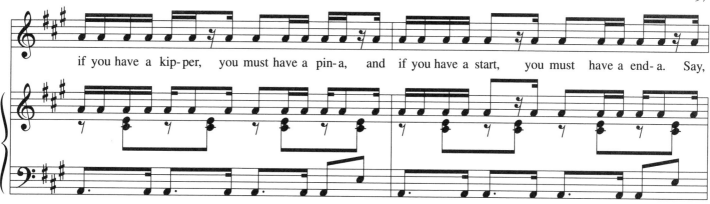

if you have a kip-per, you must have a pin-a, and if you have a start, you must have a end-a. Say,

five plus five is e-qual to ten-a, and if you have gold, you put 'em in a bin-a, and

A

if you have a roost-er, you must have a hen, now. Zung-gu-zung-gu-gu-zung-gu-zeng,— na.

N.C.

Zung-gu-zung-gu-gu-zung-gu-zeng,— na. Jump for hap-pi-ness and jump for joy,— ya.

You nev-er call Yel-low-man no boy,— ya. La-dy un-der you used to think fa-tal,— ya.

We're the Lon-don call-in' child. You nev-er call Yel-low-man no boy.—

You nev-er call John John no boy,— you no pre-dict my life was wild,— ya.

A   C   A   C

Zung - gu-zung - gu-gu-zung-gu-zeng,— *watch it!* Zung - gu - zung - gu-gu-zung - gu-zeng,— *catch it!*

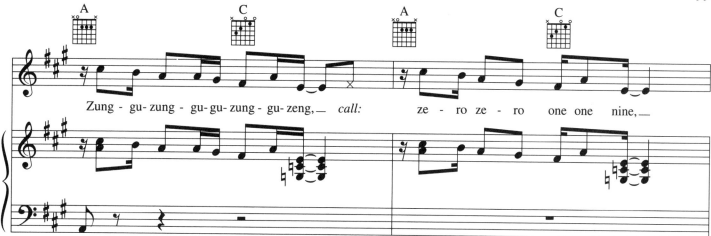

Zung - gu- zung - gu- gu- zung - gu- zeng, __ *call:* ze - ro ze - ro one one nine, __

Call Yel - low- man make you feel so fine. __ Me talk all me ly-rics, me talk-ing me my rhyme.

Me now eat lime me full of my rhyme 'cause Yel-low-man a-ma com-mit no crime, ca,

Zung - gu- zung - gu- gu- zung - gu- zeng, __ Zung - gu- zung - gu- gu- zung - gu- zeng, __ ay.

hear that wom-en of a hun-dred and ten-a. Say, all of them they of yel-low chil-dren. Say,

all of them_ they of yel-low chil-dren. So if a King-ston-a he don't have a pen-a. None of

them-a ask me all me oth-er girl-friend, true. All you mens, I have e-nough of mens, Lord.

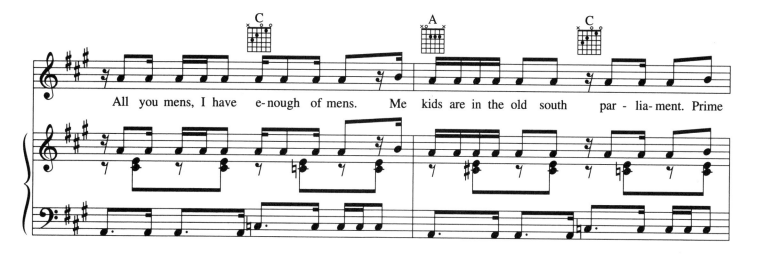

All you mens, I have e-nough of mens. Me kids are in the old south par-lia-ment. Prime

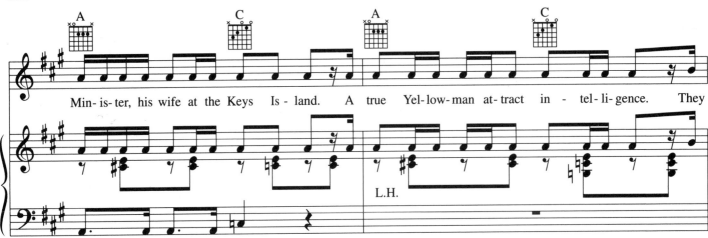

Min- is- ter, his wife at the Keys Is - land. A true Yel-low-man at-tract in - tel-li- gence. They

L.H.

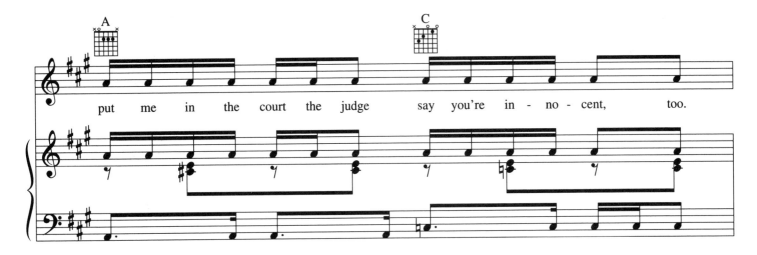

put me in the court the judge say you're in - no - cent, too.

All you mens I have e-nough of you men, ah.

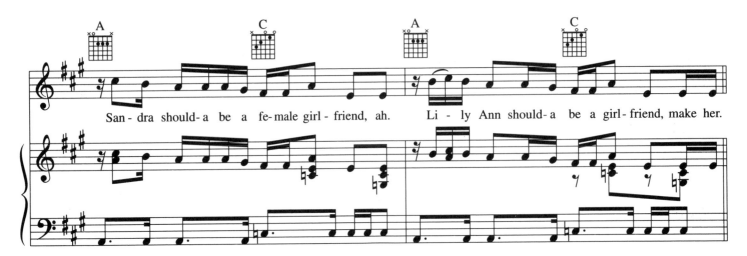

San- dra should- a be a fe-male girl- friend, ah. Li - ly Ann should- a be a girl- friend, make her.

Zung - gu-zung - gu-gu-zung - gu-zeng,__ ay. You nev-er jump for me hap-py or joy.

You nev-er call Yel-low-man no boy.__ No-bod-y take John John a toy - a.

May-be the Lord is call-ing you "Roy." Zung - gu-zung - gu-gu-zung - gu-zeng,__ *watch it-a!*

Zung gu-zung - gu-gu-zung - gu-zeng!__ You let go of my lens, your spoon eye lens.

N.C.

You give me my lens, your bot-tom eye lens. But you tell Yel-low-man, bet-ter tell him a - gain.

You live in King's Cor - ner you live near a pen - a. Say,

if you have a rules, that you must have a inn - a, and

if you have a start, you must have a end- a. Well, watch Yel- low- man come fear at them a-gain, Lord.

Zung-gu-zung-gu-gu-zung-gu-zeng,_ watch it-a! Zung-gu-zung-gu-gu-zung-gu-zeng,_ ay!

Jump for hap-pi-ness and jump for joy._ You're nev-er take the Yel-low-man free, boy_

You've nev-er take the Yel-low-man for toy._

Zung-gu-zung-gu-gu-zung-gu-zeng,_ watch it! Zung-gu-zung-gu-gu-zung-gu-zeng,_ ay.

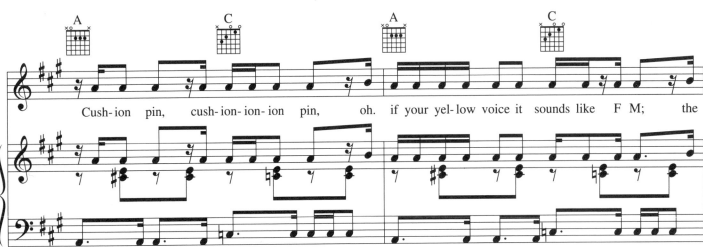

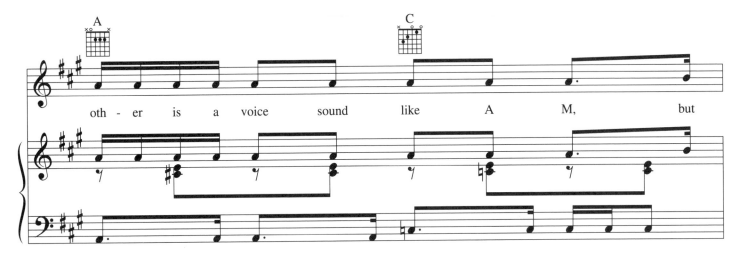

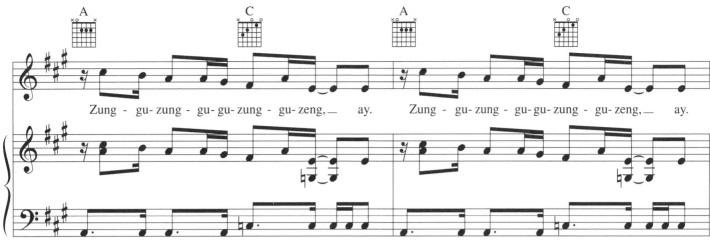

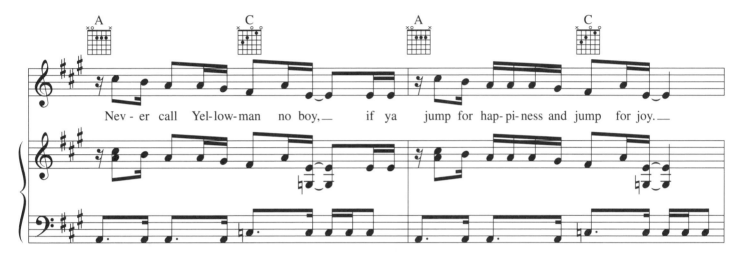

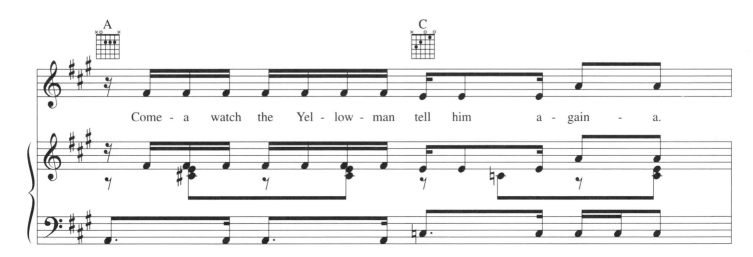

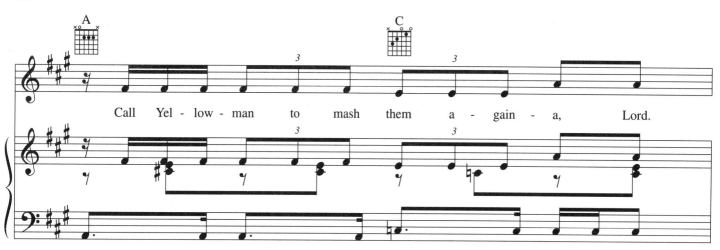

Call Yel - low - man to mash them a - gain - a, Lord.

repeat and fade